A Companion Journal to

Good Grief— I Need Relief!

A Widow's Guide to Recovering and Rejoicing

Joyce Webster

A Gift for You

_____

From:

_____

Date:

_____

A note to let you know:

_____

_____

_____

As the Lord holds you in His hands,
May the fragrance of His beauty
As the sweetness of a rose,
Bless you and envelop your friends and family.

A Companion Journal to: Good Grief—I Need Relief! A Widow's Guide to Recovering and Rejoicing

ISBN: 978-0996529310

Scripture quotations are taken from the King James Bible. Abbreviations of the books of the Bible may be found listed with the index in the front of Bibles. If they are not listed there, the general rule is the first two letters of most books are used.

Editor: Becky Towne
Cover Design: Delia Dobbs
Interior Design: Amber Smart

At the time of publication, internet addresses, email addresses, and phone numbers in this book were accurate. They are provided as a resource, and all content may not be endorsed or the permanence guaranteed by this author.

This journal is a Companion to the book

Good Grief— I Need Relief!

A Widow's Guide to Recovering and Rejoicing

Joyce Webster

This Journal records the lives of

———————————————————————

whose marriage began on

———————————————

I began writing our stories in this journal on

———————————————

and finished on

———————————————

Here is our wedding picture which I treasure,

or one of my favorites taken on

_____

As the Lord held us in His comforting hands,
May you, my descendants,
Lead your children to trust in His everlasting love
So that one day we will live together in Heaven.
God bless you and your home.

Dedication

Thanks to my wonderful children and their spouses, Pam and Kevin Nance, Michelle and Bobby Varner, Jonathan and Michelle Webster, and David and Charise Webster, for having listening ears, open hearts, and allowing me to grieve in my unique way. I am blessed beyond measure. I feel your love and appreciate your unconditional support; I love you back!

Contents

Part Three: LOOKING FORWARD

Part Four: LOOKING UP

Acknowledgements

Thank you, Jim Hills, for reigniting a love for writing in me, and pushing me to attend the writing conference that changed my life. David Sanford, your classes on publishing and personal encouragement made this book happen. I am grateful to both of you for believing in me when I didn't.

A Christian writer always needs friends to hold up their hands when they feel faint. I had such a prayer team; I thank you so much for your wonderful support. God bless each of you for lifting my needs up to the throne: Wanda Brittain, Glenn and Delia Dobbs, Dona Erquiaga, Tammy Garza, Sherry Griffin, Mindy Hyberg, Carol Keister, Haruna McKittrick, Barbara Morse, and Jeanne Williams.

Thank you, Becky Towne, for your interest in my project, well founded suggestions and capable editing of my journal.

Amber Smart, you came with high recommendations and lived up to them with your interior design. Many thanks.

Delia Dobbs, my sister-in-law and the sister I never had, thank you for your hard work on the cover and your professional advice. I couldn't have made it without you.

I am grateful for your sage advice, my brother, advisor, and confidant, Glenn Dobbs. Thank you for rejoicing with me over small and major milestones, and for letting me interrupt your life so many times when I needed you. You and Delia are the greatest!

INTRODUCTION

$\mathcal{D}$ear Widow,

This journal is designed to be used with the companion book *Good—Grief, I Need Relief! A Widow's Guide to Recovering and Rejoicing.* Basic grief information is located there plus journaling questions. This journal includes extra questions and space for complete answers rather than abbreviated ones.

Journaling isn't the same as writing a novel or a non-fiction book, and it doesn't require attending a special class. It's simply telling your husband's and your life's stories to leave a legacy for coming generations so they will know some unique facts about you—and not just view your pictures.

Please pass this journal down to your children so they in turn can pass it on to their succeeding children that it might bless several generations.

"That the generation to come might know them, even the children which should be born; who should arise and declare them to their children: that they might set their hope in God, and not forget the works of God, but keep his commandments: and might not be as their fathers, a stubborn and rebellious generation; a generation that set not their heart aright, and whose spirit was not steadfast with God" (Ps. 78:6-8).

Although the first chapter in the companion book starts with the funeral, let's fill in some background information before that about how and where you met, where you were married, the places you lived, where you worked, and your occupations. These details make names come alive and travel on through a family without becoming black ink spots on a stale piece of paper.

Grab your pen—happy writing!

Welcome to *A Companion Journal* to *Good Grief— I Need Relief! A Widow's Guide to Recovering and Rejoicing.*

Loving Blessings from Your Widowed Friend,

Joyce Webster

Part One

Looking Back

"The memory of the just is blessed..."

(Prov. 10:7a).

In the Beginning

1. That special young man who caught your eye and later became your husband, where did you first meet him? Share that experience.

_____

_____

_____

_____

_____

_____

_____

_____

_____

_____

2. How long did you date before you became engaged?

   _____

3. How long were you engaged before you were married?

   _____

4. When and where were you married?

   _____

5. Describe your wedding day by telling an unusual happening or some "Ah, Ha, or Oh, no!" moments.

   _____

   _____

   _____

   _____

   _____

   _____

   _____

6. What was unusual or unique about the first place that you lived and called home?

   _____

   _____

_____

_____

_____

_____

7. How many different places have you lived?

_____

8. Name the states or foreign countries where you lived and give the dates if that information is available.

_____

_____

_____

_____

_____

9. Was there something in either of your childhoods that significantly impacted your marriage?

   If yes, how did you resolve it?

_____

_____

_____

_____

_____

_____

_____

_____

_____

_____

10. Did you work as a stay-at-home mom, or outside the home?

_____

11. If you were a stay-at-home mom, did you run your own business or do something else to supplement the income? If so, describe it.

_____

_____

_____

_____

_____

_____

_____

12. If you worked outside the home, what, where, and for how long did you do it?

_____

_____

_____

_____

_____

_____

13. "Lo, children are an heritage of the LORD: and the fruit of the womb is his reward" (Ps. 127:3). How many children did the LORD bless your home with?

_____

14. What were their names in birth order? (If they are adults, include their occupations.)

_____

_____

_____

_____

_____

_____

15. Did you take your family to church or send them with someone else?

_____

16. What church/churches did you/they attend?

_____

_____

_____

_____

17. Did you and your husband attend church as children?

_____

If so, do you feel that played an important role in the way you reared your children?

_____

18. Did your family have a daily time of Bible reading and prayer? _____ Describe how you made it appealing to your young ones, and later to your teens.

_____

_____

_____

_____

_____

_____

_____

_____

_____

Consider

"Make me to go in the path of thy commandments; for therein do I delight" (Ps. 119:35).

Extra thoughts to share, just because...

Chapter One

∽ A BLEAK DAY ∽
THE FUNERAL

$\mathcal{E}$veryone's funeral circumstances are different. Experts seem to believe your grieving process will be anchored to whether your husband died instantly, as mine did, or whether he suffered for a long time. If your husband died quickly, you didn't have time to pre-grieve. If he lingered for awhile, you might have had time to think about the future and try to picture it without him. Some grief experts suggest that those who had time to pre-grieve might move forward quicker than those who didn't. Since each person grieves differently and in their own time frame, it doesn't really matter what the experts think or say.

As accurately as possible, record your experiences here.

1. When and where did your husband die?

_____

_____

_____

2. Was your husband's death expected? _____

   If so, how long did you deal with grieving issues?

   _____

   _____

3. Did you have a theme for his funeral?

   If so, what was it, and how did you determine it?

   _____

   _____

   _____

   His favorite saying, verse, or quote was:

   _____

   _____

   _____

   _____

   _____

   _____

4. What, if any, definite problems did you face during the initial funeral planning stage?

   _____

_____

_____

_____

5. Where is your husband buried, and what is on/or planned for his tombstone?

_____

_____

_____

What specific advice did a friend, funeral director, or a pastor give you, which helped and blessed you?

_____

_____

_____

6. What life changing decisions were reached as a result of your husband's funeral service?

(Did an estranged family member or friend attend and decide to rejoin the family? Etc.)

_____

_____

_____

_____

7. Did someone get saved? _____

8. How many? _____

9. Include any special directions or advice your husband gave you before he passed away.

_____

_____

_____

_____

_____

_____

_____

_____

Hug This

"Precious in the sight of the L*ord* is the death of his saints" (Ps. 116:15).

Extra thoughts to share, just because...

Chapter Two

∽ AM I GOING CRAZY? ∽
GOD TALK FROM JOB

1. Have you ever felt like you were going crazy? _____

   What situation/s made you feel that way?

   _____

   _____

   _____

   _____

2. What issues stand out in your mind that made you feel
   that you had miserable comforters?

   _____

   _____

   _____

   _____

3. In the book, we talked about how Job felt God dealt unfairly with him compared to how God treated other people. Do you empathize with him? _____

   If yes, in what way? _____

   _____

   _____

   _____

   _____

4. Do you feel abandoned and that God hasn't listened to you? _____

   Give specifics. _____

   _____

   _____

   _____

   _____

   _____

5. Job felt his family and friends withdrew from him. If you had friends withdraw from you, what reason did they give, or did you assume they no longer wanted your company?

   _____

_____

_____

_____

_____

6. Instead of constantly internalizing your situation, have you tried to help other widows in mourning?

_____

How did you reach out?

_____

_____

_____

_____

7. What advice would you like to give some of your family members so they can better understand what you are going through, or have been through?

_____

_____

_____

_____

8. Have you had **difficulty going to sleep** or **staying asleep**? _____

   Did you ever have the type of **dreams that Job** described in chapter 7?_____

   What were yours like? _____

   _____

   _____

   _____

   _____

   _____

9. Check off the things that Job complained about that apply to you and your situation:

   ❑ Have you ever been so **sleepy** that you couldn't wait to get to bed, but you couldn't go to sleep and tossed and turned all night when you did get there?

   ❑ Or have you slept and had **scary dreams** so that you dreaded night?

   ❑ Have you thought your days were filled with **no hope**?

   ❑ Have you had **anguish of spirit** and complained to God with **bitterness** in your soul?

   ❑ Are you **afraid to grieve**? Job said, "I am afraid of all my sorrows."

10. Did you **long to go back in time** to when you were younger and your life happier? _____

If your answer is yes, describe what time frame you would choose, and why. _____

_____

_____

_____

_____

_____

11. Do you feel a "**widow's stigma**" (mentioned in Isaiah 54:4) surrounding your life? _____

Explain what makes you feel that way. _____

_____

_____

_____

_____

_____

_____

_____

*C*ount on *I*t

"Behold, we count them happy which endure. Ye have heard of the patience of Job, and have seen the end of the Lord; that the Lord is very pitiful, and of tender mercy" (James 5:11).

EXTRA THOUGHTS TO SHARE, JUST BECAUSE...

Chapter Three

⁓ COMFORT ⁓
HOW OTHER WIDOWS SURVIVED

1. Your story is probably very different from the ones you read in the book, and might be a bit unusual too. In what areas did/do you struggle?

_____

_____

_____

2. Tell about your victories.

_____

_____

_____

_____

_____

_____

3. To whom did you reach out for comfort?

_____

_____

_____

_____

4. Name the main people who reached out to you and what they did that consoled your heart.

_____

_____

_____

_____

_____

5. Which of the many ideas that other widows used to move forward did you incorporate into your life?

_____

_____

_____

_____

_____

6. Did you remain faithful in your old church, or did you seek another place to worship due to difficult memories?

_____

7. In what church ministry/ministries were you involved?

_____

_____

_____

8. When you met other widows, did they seem stuck in grief or moving forward faster than you?

_____

_____

9. On a scale of 1-10, 10 meaning you are no longer grieving, where are you right now? _____

What can you do to move your number higher?

_____

_____

_____

_____

_____

10. Did/do you have some questions about the past that you need to work through? _____

If so, how did you go about it?

_____

_____

_____

_____

_____

Support

"I know, O LORD, that thy judgments are right, and that thou in faithfulness hast afflicted me. Let, I pray thee, thy merciful kindness be for my comfort, according to thy word unto thy servant. Let thy tender mercies come unto me, that I may live: for thy law is my delight" (Ps. 119:75-77).

Extra thoughts to share, just because...

Chapter Four

∽ TRAVELING ∽
GREAT AS A COUPLE,
DAUNTING AS A SINGLE

1. What states and countries have you visited, both as a couple and after his death, as a single?

_____

_____

_____

_____

_____

_____

_____

_____

_____

_____

2. How did you financially prepare for your trips (e.g. by saving monthly, borrowing, using air miles, or gifted by a friend)?

_____

_____

_____

_____

_____

_____

_____

_____

3. Where did you go on your most pleasant trip?

_____

_____

_____

_____

_____

_____

_____

4. What made it memorable?

_____

_____

_____

_____

_____

_____

5. Where would you like to revisit?

_____

_____

_____

_____

_____

_____

6. Did you go somewhere with a family member after your husband died?

_____

7. When, where and with whom did you go?

_____

8. What future trip/trips would you consider, and who might travel with you?

_____

_____

_____

_____

_____

_____

_____

_____

9. What places remain on your bucket list?

_____

_____

_____

_____

_____

_____

10. What pleasant memories emerge when you think of going on a picnic or driving to a grandparent's home out of town?

_____

_____

_____

_____

_____

SHARE

Share your memories with the Lord and rejoice together for the times that you enjoyed on your trips, whether they were exotic, to a grocery store, or a ball game. Remember the games you played and the music you sang together or listened to as you traveled. Grasp and hold them; they are the ticket to your memory bank.

Tell Him

"I will praise thee, O Lord my God, with all my heart: and I will glorify thy name for evermore" (Ps. 86:12).

Extra thoughts to share, just because...

_____

_____

_____

_____

_____

_____

_____

_____

_____

_____

_____

_____

_____

_____

_____

_____

_____

Chapter Five

∽ HEALTH ∽
HOW'S YOURS?

1. What particular health issue/issues did you have before your husband died?

_____

_____

_____

_____

_____

_____

2. Were these issues stress related, age related, or inherited?

_____

_____

3. After his death, what other health issues developed that required a change in your lifestyle?

_____

_____

_____

_____

4. What is the greatest health problem you battle right now? Are you making progress and improving?

_____

_____

5. What research have you done to learn if there is a new method, treatment, or prescription medicine that might benefit you?

_____

_____

_____

_____

6. What change in your body shape or size have you realized since you became a widow?

_____

7. Are you pleased with your self-image? If not, what have you determined to do to correct it?

_____

_____

_____

_____

8. Did you have an issue with eating when you began to eat alone? _____

What did you do that was helpful or solved it?

_____

_____

_____

_____

_____

9. What exercise program did you implement if you didn't already have one? _____

_____

_____

_____

_____

10. Describe what you try to do each day to ward off dementia by learning new things.

_____

_____

_____

_____

_____

Ponder

"What? Know ye not that your body is the temple of the Holy Ghost which is in you, which ye have of God, and ye are not your own? For ye are bought with a price: therefore glorify God in your body, and in your spirit, which are God's" (1 Cor. 6:19-20).

EXTRA THOUGHTS TO SHARE, JUST BECAUSE...

Chapter Six

∽ SLEEP, REST, & NAPS ∾
BRING THEM ON

 $\mathcal{C}$ an you usually accomplish most of your to-do list or the projects you have planned when you get enough sleep or a nap? If not, it's time to reevaluate; do you expect too much from yourself?

1. How many hours of rest do you think you need to feel your best? _____

2. If you don't get enough rest, how does it tend to affect you (e.g. feeling foggy brained, easily annoyed)?

   _____

   _____

   _____

   _____

3. Do you have your bedroom set up so that you relax when you walk in?_____

What plans do you have to make it more beautiful or relaxing?

_____

_____

_____

_____

_____

4. When you have friends or family in overnight do you sleep better? _____

   If yes, why do you think that is so?

   _____

   _____

   _____

   _____

   _____

5. When the sun fades and the solar lights glow in your yard, do you find yourself sad and allow loneliness to invade your home? _____

   How about thinking back on the positive things that you did or that happened to you today instead? Or choose a memory filled with happy thoughts/things you used to enjoy together with your husband. Name a couple here:

_____

_____

_____

_____

_____

6. If you fall asleep watching a movie at home and then can't get to sleep when you go to bed, what can you do to prevent it from happening next time? (e.g. exercise while you're watching, start watching earlier)?

_____

_____

7. If you are insecure by yourself after dark, what measures have you taken to secure your perimeters?

_____

_____

_____

8. The book suggests you pray before you go to sleep and thank the Lord for at least five blessings from the day. It's also a great help to ask the Lord to relax your mind and give you a peaceful sleep. Mention the

routine you have found helpful before you get into bed. (Eating a certain thing, drinking hot tea, taking a warm shower, lighting a candle, using lotion, etc.)

_____

_____

_____

_____

_____

_____

9. How do you prepare for the next day? (Lay out clothes, make a list, etc.)

_____

_____

_____

10. Does company energize you or deplete your energy and make you grumpy?

_____

11. How can you overcome this situation?

_____

_____

_____

_____

_____

_____

12. Have you or your husband ever had a demon possession experience in your home during the night?

_____

If so, what did you do to overcome it?

_____

_____

_____

_____

Rest Assured

"When thou liest down, thou shalt not be afraid: yea, thou shalt lie down, and thy sleep shall be sweet" (Prov. 3:24).

Extra thoughts to share, just because...

PART TWO

Looking Around

"And all things, whatsoever ye shall ask in prayer,
believing, ye shall receive"
(Matt. 21:22).

Chapter Seven

∽ A PRAYER PARTNER ∽
DO YOU HAVE ONE?

1. Did you and your husband pray together? _____

   What was your routine, and what special answers stand out in your mind?

   _____

   _____

   _____

   _____

   _____

   _____

   _____

   _____

2. Whom has the Lord brought into your path that you have been able to share with your heart-felt prayer requests?

   _____

3. Is she/he a new friend? _____

   If so, where and when did you meet?

   _____

   _____

   _____

   _____

4. If it is someone you have known for a long time, record how long you have known this special friend and why you feel comfortable sharing your heart with them.

   _____

   _____

5. What topics have you discussed, cried, and prayed about together?

   _____

   _____

   _____

_____

_____

_____

_____

6. What prayer requests can you list that were answered as a result?

_____

_____

_____

_____

_____

7. What would you like to tell your family about your prayer life that they might incorporate?

_____

_____

_____

_____

_____

8. Who in your life instigated your prayer habits?

_____

_____

_____

_____

_____

_____

9. Did your parents pray with you as a child and encourage you to pray on your own?

_____

10. What particular incident do you recall where you prayed and received a positive answer as a child which might have strengthened your faith?

_____

_____

_____

_____

_____

_____

_____

_____

_____

_____

11. Do you recall your husband sharing one with you also? _____

    If so, what and who was involved?

    _____

    _____

    _____

    _____

    _____

    _____

    _____

12. Did your family share a devotional time together during your married life? _____

    If yes, what can you share about it? (When and where, etc.)

    _____

    _____

    _____

13. If you don't have a prayer partner now, why not ask the Lord to give you a dear friend in whom you can confide. Pray the verse below, Matthew 7:7, and see what happens.

Today, *(Insert the date)* _____

I prayed and asked the Lord for a prayer partner. He answered on _____

(Date) and gave me _____

as that special friend. We have determined to pray with/for each other and to hold each other accountable. Describe how you plan to stay in touch.

_____

_____

_____

_____

_____

_____

Lean on This

"Ask, and it shall be given you; seek, and ye shall find; knock, and it shall be opened unto you: For every one that asketh receiveth; and he that seeketh findeth; and to him that knocketh it shall be opened" (Matt. 7:7).

Extra thoughts to share, just because...

Chapter Eight

❧ HOME OWNERSHIP & REPAIRS ❧ YIKES!

1. After your husband died, if you lived in a house, what was the first thing that had to be done to it?

   _____

   _____

   _____

2. Did your children or a friend help with your house repairs, or did you hire someone to do them? (If you did them yourself, I applaud you!)

   _____

   _____

   _____

3. Have you, like I, found it true that "cheapest" might be more expensive in the long run? _____

If so, share your experience.

_____

_____

_____

4. Was it necessary for you to move after your husband passed away? _____

If so, where and how did you do it?

_____

_____

_____

_____

5. What main things moved with you, and what did you put in storage, if any?

_____

_____

_____

_____

6. What did you sell?

_____

_____

_____

_____

_____

_____

_____

7. If you gave some things to family members, list them and to whom you gave them, and the date. (This might prove helpful later when you can't locate something and don't remember to whom you gave it. Use the extra pages if needed).

_____

_____

_____

_____

_____

_____

_____

_____

_____

_____

8. What future plans do you have to remodel your home?

_____

_____

_____

_____

_____

_____

9. Have you ever taken the time to dedicate your home/apartment/motor home or wherever you live, to the Lord? Even if you have lived in it for years, the Lord would be pleased to hear you pray and ask for His blessings on it.

    o   I dedicated it the first time on

    _____

    o   I will do it again on

    _____

    o   I have never blessed/dedicated my house, but today I have decided I will do it on

    _____

10. How can you use your home to bless other people? (Invite other widows in, have missionaries stay with you, etc.)

_____

_____

_____

_____

Hold This

"Peace I leave with you, my peace I give unto you: not as the world giveth, give I unto you. Let not your heart be troubled, neither let it be afraid" (John 14:27)

Extra thoughts to share, just because...

Chapter Nine

RINGS AND THINGS

1. What is your special story surrounding your wedding ring/rings? (Ex. we picked them out together, he bought them in another country, etc.)

   _____

   _____

   _____

   _____

   _____

   _____

2. Share the account of when, where and how he gave your ring to you. _____

   _____

   _____

   _____

_____

_____

_____

_____

3. How did you break the news of your engagement to your family?

_____

_____

_____

_____

_____

4. Did your husband-to-be ask your dad if he could marry you before he gave you a ring? _____

Give the details whether yes or no.

_____

_____

_____

_____

5. How long have you worn/or do you plan to wear your rings since becoming a widow?

    _____

    _____

    _____

    _____

    _____

6. What future plans do you have for your rings? (e.g. store them in a safety deposit box, reset the diamonds into a dinner ring, remount and add some different stones, make it into a necklace or earrings, give as a gift to one of your children.)

    _____

    _____

    _____

7. Do you feel that you need to confer with your family about your plans for your rings before you make a final commitment?_____

    Detail your arrangements, such as a special family get together on

    _____

    _____

CAN YOU?

Can you pray the prayer of dedication and mean
it from your heart?

PRAYER OF DEDICATION:

"Lord, we as widows dedicate the rest of our lives to
wholly following You. Thank you for loving and caring for
the small things, which loom like mountains before our
eyes when we are grieving. Help us to be pleasantly
surprised when You give us the peace and wisdom we are
searching for in such areas as rings and other things. In
Your precious name, amen."

Stop and Think

"Is anything too hard for the Lord?" (Gen. 18:14).

Extra thoughts to share, just because...

_____

_____

_____

_____

_____

_____

_____

_____

_____

_____

_____

_____

_____

_____

_____

_____

Chapter Ten

∽ LONELINESS ∽
A KILLER

1. Oswald Chambers says we should thank God for our broken heart. Why does he say that?

   _____

   _____

   _____

   _____

   _____

2. If you live alone, do you have difficulty with loneliness? _____

   When it overcomes you, if you leave the house to get relief where do you go?

   _____

   _____

   _____

3. What do you like to do there? (Go for coffee, shop, find someone to talk to)

    _____

    _____

    _____

4. Do you have a pet? _____

    What's its name and breed?

    _____

5. Did you get it before or after your husband died?

    _____

    How long have you had it? _____

6. What do you find comforting about it?

    _____

    _____

    _____

    _____

7. Does it travel with you? _____

    If not, what arrangements do you make for its care?

    _____

_____

_____

8. Does your pet keep you from entertaining like you want to? _____

9. If yes, what can you do to rectify the situation (install a pet door, purchase a kennel, take it to obedience school, etc.)?

_____

_____

_____

10. Check each of the following that has proven effective for you to conquer your loneliness, then add anything else that has helped you.

    ❑ "I go to Facebook to talk with people."

    ❑ "I sit and cuddle my cats."

    ❑ "Once in awhile I allow myself time to have a pity party, and I cry and talk to God."

    ❑ "I listen to and sing songs that God uses to remind me that He cares."

    ❑ "I don't always read the Bible, or listen to Christian music, or pray, but I enjoy getting emails from GriefShare, and save the really good ones and read them over and over."

❑ "I invite grandkids to sleep over, make crafts, or bake."

❑ "Sometimes I just lie down and rest."

❑ "Occasionally I wear my deceased husband's shirt or my dad's."

_____

_____

_____

Victory

"And the peace of God, which passeth all understanding, shall keep your hearts and minds through Christ Jesus" (Phil. 4:7).

Extra thoughts to share, just because...

_____

_____

_____

_____

_____

_____

_____

_____

_____

_____

_____

_____

_____

_____

_____

_____

_____

Chapter Eleven

∽ EMOTIONS ∽
A ROLLER COASTER RIDE

1. Have you ever had an emotional flashback since your husband died? _____

   If so, where were you and what "triggered" the moment?

   _____

   _____

   _____

2. What did you do to compensate?

   _____

   _____

   _____

   _____

   _____

3. What mountaintop and valley experiences have you gone through?

_____

_____

_____

_____

_____

_____

_____

_____

4. Do you feel like you can't go on alone? _____

Explain why.

_____

_____

_____

_____

_____

_____

5. Are you involved in some worthwhile projects as helping someone, or are you hiding in your house hating to face the day?

_____

_____

_____

_____

_____

6. Is your spiritual life famished or flourishing?_____

By that you mean... _____

_____

_____

_____

_____

7. What in particular seems to be overwhelming you? (repairs, paperwork, etc.)

_____

_____

_____

_____

_____

8. If you have kept another journal, share some of your important thoughts on your road to recovery.

_____

_____

_____

_____

_____

_____

_____

_____

_____

9. Have you actually taken time to grieve by going over the different stages of your life that you shared with your husband? _____

Write down some of your thoughts as a result of your studies. _____

_____

_____

_____

_____

_____

_____

_____

_____

_____

_____

10. What things do you see couples doing that make it difficult for you to watch? Give an example.

_____

_____

_____

_____

_____

_____

_____

If you have never kept a journal, why not buy one, a notebook, or tablet, or use your computer, (anything will work, it doesn't have to be expensive), and start tracking your journey by writing down your feelings either by the day, or the week? You will be amazed when you look back in future years and relive some incidents you might have forgotten.

Overwhelmed?

"Hear my cry, O God; attend unto my prayer. From the end of the earth will I cry unto thee, when my heart is overwhelmed: lead me to the rock that is higher than I. For thou hast been a shelter for me, and a strong tower from the enemy. I will abide in thy tabernacle for ever: I will trust in the covert of thy wings. Selah" (Ps. 61:1-4).

Extra thoughts to share, just because...

Chapter Twelve

∽ HOLIDAYS & ANNIVERSARIES ∽
COPING WITHOUT RETREATING TO
A DESERT ISLAND!

1. Which holidays and holiday traditions stand out to you?

   _____

   _____

   _____

   _____

   _____

2. Do you still celebrate them in the same way you did with your husband? _____

   If not, how have you changed your holidays?

   _____

   _____

_____

_____

_____

_____

_____

3. Did you ever make homemade gifts for your children?

_____

What outstanding memory do you have of Christmas?

_____

_____

_____

_____

_____

_____

4. How would you change the memories that you have of your holidays if you could go back and revisit them?

_____

_____

_____

_____

_____

_____

5. What would you want to freeze about the past and never have it change? _____

   Why? _____

   _____

   _____

   _____

   _____

   _____

6. What special things did you traditionally do with your husband on your anniversary?

   _____

   _____

   _____

   _____

   _____

7. What have you done to treat yourself to something unique since his death?

_____

_____

_____

_____

_____

_____

8. What have you done to keep his memory alive for your children and grandkids?

_____

_____

_____

_____

_____

9. Do you think you make your family feel bad when you talk about your husband, or is it a relief and release for all involved? Describe what you do.

_____

_____

_____

_____

_____

10. Is your home still decorated the way you had it when your husband was alive? _____

If not, describe how you changed it.

_____

_____

_____

_____

_____

_____

Our Strength

"The LORD upholdeth all that fall, and raiseth up
all those that be bowed down" (Ps. 145:14).

Extra thoughts to share, just because...

_____

_____

_____

_____

_____

_____

_____

_____

_____

_____

_____

_____

_____

_____

_____

PART THREE

Looking Forward

"The steps of a good man are ordered by the LORD: and he delighteth in his way"
(Ps. 37:23).

Chapter Thirteen

∽ DATING AND REMARRIAGE ∽
WHAT'S THIS?

$\mathcal{S}$tormy days might be ahead if you decide to start dating without letting your family know so that they can be prepared to see you with someone other than your former husband and/or their father. A wise widow gets counsel regarding someone who might want to date her. Your pastor is a good one to seek advice from as he might know something about that person that he can't share, but it could save you heartache in the future if you heed his advice not to see him.

1. Thoughts you might like to share with your family members to let them know how you feel about dating and remarriage include:

_____

_____

_____

_____

_____

_____

_____

_____

2. How do you feel about the suggestions that people have given you regarding a possible future husband?

_____

_____

_____

_____

_____

_____

3. How long after your husband's death would you think you might be ready to date if you choose to?

_____

4. If you have chosen to date, how long did it take before you felt comfortable accepting a date?

_____

5. Where did you or could you find an eligible man (online, at church, social function, former friend, etc.)?

_____

_____

6. What qualities do you want to see in a date before you would consider him becoming your second husband?

_____

_____

_____

7. Did you and your husband discuss remarriage before he died? _____

Explain: _____

_____

_____

_____

8. What thoughts has your family expressed about you dating or remarrying?

_____

_____

_____

9. Have they made a suggestion about someone they do not want you to date? _____

    Why do you think they feel that way?

    _____

    _____

    _____

10. Has someone you know remarried after their husband died and they gave you some helpful information regarding a possible date/mate?

    _____

    _____

    _____

    _____

Be Assured

"For the woman which hath an husband is bound by the law to her husband so long as he liveth; but if the husband be dead, she is loosed from the law of her husband" (Rom. 7:2).

EXTRA THOUGHTS TO SHARE, JUST BECAUSE...

Chapter Fourteen

∽ MISSING INGREDIENTS ∽
THE SEARCH IS ON

1. Dear widow, considering the list in the book, what ingredients are missing in your life that gave you a savory past? Post your special list here:

- _____

- _____

- _____

- _____

- _____

- _____

- _____

- _____

- _____

- _____

2. What ten things did you love most about your husband?

1. _____

2. _____

3. _____

4. _____

5. _____

6. _____

7. _____

8. _____

9. _____

10. _____

3. What positive traits best describe your husband that you would like to share with your future generations?

_____

_____

_____

_____

_____

_____

4. Did he have a negative trait that you would rather forget? (Yes, we want everyone to think he was perfect, but there is only One who is!)

_____

_____

_____

_____

_____

5. Do the same steps for yourself. (Positive and negative)

_____

_____

_____

_____

_____

_____

_____

_____

_____

_____

_____

_____

6. What do you plan to do with things that you feel might need a special home after you have them for a period of time? (Such as his extra Bibles, special awards, etc.)

_____

_____

_____

_____

_____

7. Can you think of something your husband dreamed of doing but he never had the opportunity to accomplish before his death?

_____

_____

_____

_____

_____

8. Is there something that you can do to make it happen?

_____

_____

_____

_____

9. What regret do you have that centers around something you might have done to make him happy before he died?

_____

_____

_____

Commit to It

"The LORD also will be a refuge for the oppressed, a refuge in times of trouble" (Ps. 9:9).

EXTRA THOUGHTS TO SHARE, JUST BECAUSE...

Chapter Fifteen

SCRIPTURAL PROMISES FOR WIDOWS

1. The book mentions many promises. How many have you claimed? _____

    _____

    _____

2. Which one/ones blessed you the most?

    _____

    _____

    _____

    _____

    _____

    _____

3. Some promises include: "...He _____
    the fatherless and widow" (Ps. 146:9).

4. What two things does the Lord promise to give the fatherless and widows in (Deut. 10:18)?

- _____

- _____

5. Psalm 146:9 says the Lord relieves the widows. How have you applied that promise to your life?

_____

_____

_____

_____

_____

_____

6. Have you ever had someone falsely accuse you and the LORD took your part? (Mal.3:5). ___ Explain how it came about and how you were justified.

_____

_____

_____

_____

_____

_____

7. Widows were encouraged in Deuteronomy 24 to glean. Have you considered doing so if your health allows it? _____

   If you have, tell about your experience.

   _____

   _____

   _____

   _____

   _____

8. What story have you told a friend, family member, or a widowed friend about how much God loves them?

   _____

   _____

   _____

   _____

   _____

   _____

   _____

   _____

   _____

9. After listening to a widow's particular problem, have you shared one of the verses with her? Which one brought her comfort?

_____

_____

_____

_____

_____

10. We are warned in Numbers 30:8 that if we vow something we are to keep that vow if we don't have a husband to break it. Can you think of a particular vow you made before your husband died (such as the issue of remarrying,) that he never disannulled?

_____

Tell your family about it.

_____

_____

_____

_____

_____

_____

A Caring Widow

"Cause me to hear thy lovingkindness in the morning; for in thee do I trust: cause me to know the way wherein I should walk; for I lift up my soul unto thee" (Ps. 143:8).

Extra thoughts to share, just because...

_____

_____

_____

_____

_____

_____

_____

_____

_____

_____

_____

_____

_____

_____

_____

Chapter Sixteen

FINANCIAL TIPS
FOR SURVIVING WIDOWHOOD

1. When your husband died, by what percentage did your previous income increase or decrease?

   _____

2. As a result, what could you do or not do?

   _____

   _____

   _____

   _____

   _____

3. Did you have to cut back on something? _____

   If yes, describe how you did it.

   _____

   _____

_____

_____

_____

_____

_____

4. How did you learn to be resourceful and stay within
   your budget (e.g. reading articles online, going to the
   library, talking to friends about tips on saving,
   couponing)? _____

   _____

   _____

   _____

   _____

   _____

   _____

5. How did the Lord meet your needs in particular,
   special ways?

   _____

   _____

   _____

_____

_____

_____

_____

_____

6. Were you already employed? _____

If so, where did you work and for how long?

_____

_____

_____

_____

_____

7. Did you opt to change to another job situation, or continue as you were? Why? (Needed fresh start, decided self-employment was the right direction, etc.)

_____

_____

_____

_____

_____

8. How have you prepared for the future by setting aside an emergency fund?

_____

_____

_____

_____

9. If you inventoried your estate, what did you find you could live without, and how did you go about turning it into cash?

_____

_____

_____

_____

_____

_____

10. Just as I experienced, what things have you managed that overwhelmed you—but were necessary because they had your name written on them?

_____

_____

_____

_____

_____

_____

It's True

"And it shall come to pass, that before they call, I will answer: and while they are yet speaking, I will hear" (Isa. 65:24).

EXTRA THOUGHTS TO SHARE, JUST BECAUSE...

Chapter Seventeen

A Widow's Answered Prayers

1. What special prayers has the Lord answered for you?

_____

_____

_____

_____

_____

_____

2. What lessons did you learn through your experiences?

_____

_____

_____

_____

_____

3. Share an incident when the timing proved it was a "God thing" and it also answered your prayer.

_____

_____

_____

_____

_____

_____

4. If you prayed for a neighbor, how has the Lord allowed you to reach out to them and impact their life?

_____

_____

_____

_____

_____

_____

5. What occurred in your life which allowed someone else to minister to you and answered a prayer at the same time?

_____

_____

_____

_____

_____

_____

6. What storm in your life has the Lord used to teach you something special and resulted in an answered prayer? _____

_____

_____

_____

_____

_____

7. Share how the Lord allowed you to do something that solved one of your own requests. _____

_____

_____

_____

_____

_____

_____

8. What unusual answer to prayer have you experienced? _____

_____

_____

_____

_____

_____

9. What major request are you still waiting on?

_____

_____

_____

_____

10. How can you use these answers to prayer for good in the future (e.g. share with grandkids, write and submit them for publication, prepare them for a Bible study group with a worksheet, etc.)?

_____

_____

_____

_____

_____

_____

_____

_____

Blessed

"Every day will I bless thee; and I will praise thy name
for ever and ever" (Ps. 145:2).

EXTRA THOUGHTS TO SHARE, JUST BECAUSE...

Chapter Eighteen

STEPPING INTO A
NEW LIFE'S PURPOSE

1. What special way can you welcome a "newbie" widow
    to your neighborhood? (There were some ideas in the
    book.)

    _____

    _____

    _____

    _____

    _____

2. How can you help a friend who recently joined the
    ranks of widowhood? (If she is out of your area, try a
    search on www.GriefShare.com to see if a grief group
    exists in her town).

    _____

    _____

_____

_____

_____

_____

3. Which idea/ideas from this chapter can you make a reality in your life? _____

_____

_____

_____

_____

_____

4. What is the first step you need to take?

_____

_____

_____

_____

5. How soon can you start? _____

_____

6. Share your thoughts on your new purpose in life.

_____

_____

_____

_____

7. "How Can We Live a Profitable Life?" suggests six things to help cope with depression. List the ones you've used successfully.

_____

_____

_____

_____

_____

8. Check which ideas might work for you from this "More Practical Ways for Widows to Make a Difference," list.

❑ Invite your neighbor to church

❑ Donate your husband's musical instruments to a missionary who runs an orphanage

❑ Online classes

❑ Work on a church bus route

❑ Send funds to help a national missionary recover from a natural disaster

9. Number six under "Top Ten Tips for New Widows" says to look forward to something fun. How and what fun thing have you incorporated into your life that makes you anticipate and look forward to it?

_____

_____

_____

_____

10. If you have found interaction with a good grief group helpful, comment on it:

_____

_____

_____

_____

Marching Orders

So teach us to number our days, that we may apply our hearts unto wisdom" (Ps. 90:12).

Extra thoughts to share, just because...

Part Four

Looking Up

"For as the heavens are higher than the earth,
so are my ways higher than your ways,
and my thoughts than your thoughts" (Isaiah 55:9).

Chapter Nineteen

∽ SPIRITUAL HELPS ∽
WHO DOESN'T NEED THEM?

1. Record your thoughts regarding your walk with the Lord (e.g. sporadic, faithful, dynamic, cold, etc.):

   _____

   _____

   _____

   _____

2. What progress do you plan to see soon? (e.g. I plan to study the book of _____, memorize some verses, pick a subject such as "widow" and learn as much as I can, etc.)

   _____

   _____

   _____

_____

_____

_____

_____

3. What deep hunger are you waiting for the Lord to fill in your life?

_____

_____

_____

_____

4. Have you ever been sidetracked from His presence and His Word? If so, recall how you felt and reacted.

_____

_____

_____

_____

5. What particular verses have blessed and encouraged you lately?

_____

_____

_____

_____

_____

_____

_____

6. List some verses from those mentioned in the book that you would like to memorize.

_____

_____

_____

_____

_____

7. Consider making a list of verses that you can share with other widows when you visit them.

_____

_____

_____

_____

_____

8. "Bless the Lord, O my soul, and forget not all His benefits" (Ps. 103:2). What benefits can you name since you became a widow?

_____

_____

_____

_____

_____

9. "He healeth the broken in heart, and bindeth up their wounds" (Ps. 147:3). How has the Lord shown you the truth of this verse, that He can heal the broken in heart?

_____

_____

_____

_____

10. "Save me, O God; for the waters are come in unto my soul. I sink in deep mire, where there is no standing: I am come into deep waters, where the floods overflow me. I am weary of my crying: my throat is dried: mine eyes fail while I wait for my God" (Ps. 69:1-3). If you cry easily, share what triggers your tears.

_____

$\mathcal{B}e\ \mathcal{A}ssured$

"I waited patiently for the LORD; and he inclined unto me, and heard my cry. He brought me up also out of an horrible pit, out of the miry clay, and set my feet upon a rock, and established my goings. And he hath put a new song in my mouth, even praise unto our God: many shall see it, and fear, and shall trust in the LORD" (Ps. 40:1-3).

EXTRA THOUGHTS TO SHARE, JUST BECAUSE...

Chapter Twenty

SPIRITUAL WARFARE

$\mathcal{D}$ear widow, what situation in your life is binding you? Does it include bitterness, hatred, or denial? Whatever it is, I give you permission to do what the Lord wants for you. Free yourself by confessing and forsaking whatever issue is holding you back.

1. Who or what stands between you and peace?

   _____

   _____

   _____

   _____

2. Liberating the circumstance or person through forgiveness will liberate you. Describe how and when you plan to do it.

   _____

   _____

_____

_____

_____

_____

3. Since sharing some personal information might not be what you want to leave in a legacy, why don't you take a separate piece of paper and write out the situation/situations that you want closure on, and when you have finished, pray through your list or situation. Ask the Lord to terminate the snare that Satan, the king of terrors, has laid for you. Claim the blood of Christ to free you.

_____

God bless you as you take this important step in your life that will allow you to breathe more easily, sleep better, and take the next step in your new life—freedom.

4. Some widows find they have a harder time going to church since their husband cannot attend with them. If that is your case, prayerfully consider what steps you can take to overcome it, and write out your victory plan.

_____

_____

_____

_____

_____

_____

5. What has Satan used in your life to try to get you to give up going to church such as: disorganization, running late, no decent clothing, traveling, too busy, company, etc.?

_____

_____

_____

_____

_____

_____

6. May our children say to their children, "Grandma loved the Lord, and even after Grandpa died, she attended church faithfully—as long as her health allowed." Is this a part of your philosophy?

_____

_____

_____

_____

7. What good subtle signals are you giving out?

_____

_____

_____

_____

8. What organizational steps have you begun to hold your flag higher? (Refer to **"Grandma Time"** and **"Subtle Signals"** if you are stuck).

_____

_____

_____

_____

_____

_____

9. If you want to let the Holy Spirit search your soul and reveal to you what stands between you and the blessings the Lord is waiting to pour out on your life, how can you begin?

_____

_____

_____

_____

_____

10. What safeguards have you instituted in your life to uphold your moral purity?

_____

_____

_____

_____

_____

Carry His Torch

"Cause me to hear thy lovingkindness in the morning; for in thee do I trust: cause me to know the way wherein I should walk; for I lift up my soul unto thee" (Ps. 143:8).

EXTRA THOUGHTS TO SHARE, JUST BECAUSE...

Chapter Twenty-One

IS THERE LIFE AFTER DEATH?

By Missionary Paul Williams

1. Do you agree with Webster's 1828 American Dictionary that life ceases when we die? _____

   Why or why not?

   _____

   _____

   _____

   _____

   _____

2. When our children cause a rift between us and we do our best to offer a peaceable solution, they can either accept the peace offering and ask for forgiveness so the relationship can be restored, or reject it and continue on their own path which would widen the

rift. What way have you applied that to your own situation with the Lord?

_____

_____

_____

_____

_____

3. Have you asked the Lord to forgive your sins and trust Him by faith to give you eternal life? If so, what was the date?_____

What were the circumstances, and where did this take place? (Record it so that your family can share in the details of this life changing action.)

_____

_____

_____

_____

_____

_____

_____

_____

_____

_____

4. Were you baptized following your conversion?

_____

If yes, where and when? _____

_____

5. How did your decision change your life? (e.g. I wanted to read the Bible more, I was convicted of _____

_____

in my life and prayed to have it eradicated.)

6. If your husband shared his salvation experience with you, relate it here so your family can rejoice also.

_____

_____

_____

_____

_____

_____

7. Make a list of the churches that you and your husband attended through the years and where they were located so your children can research them and even attend if they so choose.

_____

_____

_____

_____

_____

_____

_____

8. List positions of service each of you held in the church if any: (e.g. Sunday school teacher, bus worker, nursery worker, etc.)

_____

_____

_____

_____

_____

_____

_____

_____

9. Name a pastor who stands out in your mind and what they or his wife did to make a lasting impression on your life.

_____

_____

_____

_____

10. If you have never chosen to accept the Lord as your Savior, won't you do it right now and record the date here.

_____

God's Wish

"That all the people of the earth might know the hand of the LORD, that it is mighty: that ye might fear the LORD your God for ever" (Josh. 4:24).

EXTRA THOUGHTS TO SHARE, JUST BECAUSE...

Chapter Twenty-Two

∽ THE FUTURE ∽
WHERE ARE MY SUNGLASSES?

$\mathcal{B}$eing a widow can be exciting as well as exhausting. I pray your days are becoming easier and you can see through the fog that once clouded your horizon. Although the hurt in your heart is always there, it does dim with time. If you aren't there yet, just know that happier days lie ahead, and they will come. Isn't that good news?

1. In a couple of sentences, write out the vision the Lord has placed on your heart for the horizon of your tomorrows. I pray that you execute His plan and purpose for your life. (Perhaps a new business? Remarriage? Traveling? Retraining? Writing?) My new plans include:

_____

_____

_____

_____

_____

_____

_____

_____

_____

2. List what project/s makes you jump out of bed and get started (working in your yard, writing, helping a neighbor, getting your new business set up, etc.)?

_____

_____

_____

_____

_____

_____

_____

3. What favorite spot calls you when it's time for your devotions?

_____

_____

_____

_____

4. What dream do you believe the Lord has for you to complete? Do not give up on it. Name it and do it! I believe the Lord wants me to

_____

_____

_____

_____

_____

_____

By His grace, I plan to do just that!

5. Here are some suggestions for reaching out and helping others. Check the ones that might be of interest to you.

❑ If your church doesn't have a widows group, what positive influence can you have to start one?

❑ Can you volunteer to help a widow with grocery purchases or a ride to a food bank?

- ❑ Can you network with other widows in your area or state and encourage fun meetings to develop new friendships?

- ❑ Does a widow need help with mediation with her family?

- ❑ Are you able to take her to a lawyer to have her will updated?

- ❑ How about helping her get her house ready to sell?

- ❑ Does she need help going through boxes that have been stored?

- ❑ Can you pick up medications for her?

- ❑ Would you enjoy visiting some widows in a nursing or rehab facility?

- ❑ Could you listen to a shut in widow's story and then pray and share Bible verses with her?

- ❑ If your church provides meals for shut ins, could you be a driver and help deliver them?

- ❑ Or could you help cook the meals?

- ❑ Can you bake some cookies for a bus route?

- ❑ When missionaries visit your church, could you house them?

- ❑ Could you start a church library?

❑ How about introducing the GriefShare recovery program to your pastor and if he agrees, help him launch it?

6. Which of the suggestions can you start working on right away?

_____

_____

_____

_____

_____

7. What widowed friend can you help reach one of her future goals?

_____

8. How will you do that?

_____

_____

_____

_____

_____

9. Include one of your favorite pictures of your husband and you that makes you feel warm and fuzzy. Include information as when, where and the occasion.

Place the picture and anything else about your husband that you have not had room to include in this journal on the last EXTRA THOUGHTS TO SHARE, JUST BECAUSE...page.

Enjoy These

"Teach me to do thy will; for thou art my God: thy spirit is good; lead me into the land of uprightness" (Ps. 143:10).

"Cause me to hear thy lovingkindness in the morning; for in thee do I trust: cause me to know the way wherein I should walk; for I lift up my soul unto thee" (Ps. 143:8).

Extra thoughts to share, just because...

_____

_____

_____

_____

_____

_____

_____

_____

_____

_____

_____

_____

_____

_____

_____

_____

_____

Chapter Twenty-Three

✑ LEGACY ✑
THE REST OF THE STORY

I feel sure you and your husband left a wonderful legacy. Take time to tell his and your story so that future generations might realize their heritage.

1. What would you like for them to know about him?

_____

_____

_____

_____

_____

_____

_____

_____

_____

_____

2. What would you like for your family to know about you?

_____

_____

_____

_____

_____

_____

_____

_____

_____

_____

3. How would you describe your husband for your grandchildren? Of course he was handsome, so do mention his hair, eyes, etc., but also his character traits such as: generous, kind, never met a stranger, loved helping others, a fix-it man, etc.

_____

_____

_____

_____

_____

_____

_____

_____

_____

_____

_____

4. Give some examples of things he enjoyed doing. (e.g. gardening, mechanical, hunting, fishing, etc.):

_____

_____

_____

_____

_____

_____

5. List his accomplishments and any special awards he received (military, a doctorate, etc.) or whatever might apply to your special man.

_____

_____

_____

_____

_____

_____

_____

_____

_____

_____

_____

6. What ten positive words best describe your husband?

1. _____

2. _____

3. _____

4. _____

5. _____

6. _____

7. _____

8. _____

9. _____

10. _____

7. Do the same steps for yourself.

1. _____

2. _____

3. _____

4. _____

5. _____

6. _____

7. _____

8. _____

9. _____

10. _____

8. Make a list of the different places you lived and add where you and your husband worked at each one.

- We started at _____

  He worked at _____

  From _____

  to _____

  I worked at _____

  From _____

  to _____

- Then we moved to _____

  And he worked at _____

  From _____

  to _____

  I worked at _____

  From _____

  to _____

- Then we moved to _____

  And he worked at _____

  From _____

  to _____

  I worked at _____

  From _____

  to _____

If you need more room, continue on the
EXTRA THOUGHTS TO SHARE, JUST BECAUSE...

9. What special things do you enjoy doing?

_____

_____

_____

_____

_____

_____

_____

10. List any accomplishments and special awards that you received.

_____

_____

_____

_____

_____

_____

_____

_____

Consider

"The steps of a good man are ordered by the LORD: and he delighteth in his way" (Ps. 37:23).

INCLUDE ONE OF YOUR FAVORITE PICTURES OF
YOUR HUSBAND AND YOU.

WHEN:_____

WHERE: _____

OCCASION: _____

Extra thoughts to share, just because...

After you finish your journal the first time through, think back on your life and add whatever you need to complete your stories. Then as the years roll by, visit these pages again to add additional details or information. For additional helps, please visit my website:
www.rejoicewithjoyce.org. Blessings to you and yours.

_____

_____

_____

_____

_____

_____

_____

_____

_____

_____

_____

_____

_____

For further encouragement you are invited to join a closed Facebook group called, *The Widow's Zone.*

If you received a blessing from this book, would you please encourage other widows to receive the same by leaving a review on Amazon?

ABOUT JOYCE WEBSTER

Joyce Webster, a widowed missionary, retired teacher, published writer, speaker, and mother, coordinates the Grief Outreach ministry at the church she attends, Riverview Baptist Church in Pasco, Washington. Joyce was married to her childhood sweetheart Warren for forty-six years before he died instantly of a major heart attack in Tokyo, Japan. She enjoys working with widows and encourages women to rejoice in the Lord through her weekly radio devotionals, *Rejoicing with Joyce.* She is the founder and president of *Rejoicing with Joyce International,* a non-profit corporation. Connect with Joyce at www.facebook.com/joyce.webster.961, or listen to her devotional radio broadcasts at www.rejoicewithjoyce.org.

Thank you for purchasing this book. A portion of author proceeds will be given to missions projects to further the gospel around the world.

ALSO BY JOYCE WEBSTER

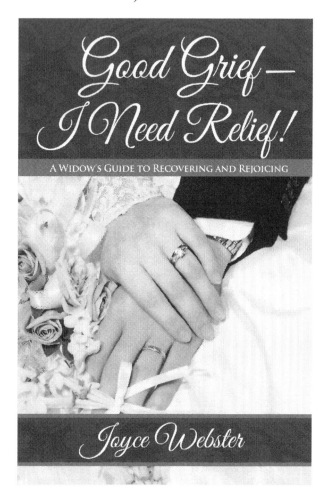

Good Grief—
I Need Relief!

A WIDOW'S GUIDE TO RECOVERING AND REJOICING

Joyce Webster

Made in the USA
Middletown, DE
22 September 2019